WITNESSES TO RACISM

WITNESSES TO RACISM

PERSONAL EXPERIENCES
OF RACIAL INJUSTICE

Edited by Lois Prebil, osf

Office for Racial Justice
Archdiocese of Chicago

acta
PUBLICATIONS

WITNESSES TO RACISM

Personal Experiences of Racial Injustice

Edited by Lois Prebil, osf

Cover photo and design by Tom A. Wright
Cover art from mural "The Last Supper to Be" by Samuel Akainyah
Text design and typesetting by Patricia Lynch

The testimonies in this book are used with the written permission of the authors.

Published by ACTA Publications, 5559 W. Howard Street, Skokie, IL 60077-2621, (800) 397-2282, www.actapublications.com

Library of Congress Catalog number: 2009936382
ISBN: 978-0-87946-415-8
Printed in the United States of Evangel Press
Year 20 19 18 17 1615 14 13 12 11 10 09
Printing 15 14 13 12 11 10 9 8 7 6 5 4 3 2 First

CONTENTS

Dedication

For all of us,
in particular for our brothers and sisters of color,
because of the ways
we have been affected by
racial injustice.

MESSAGE FROM FRANCIS CARDINAL GEORGE

Those who read my pastoral letter on racism, "Dwell in My Love," often comment on the story I relate of my childhood and the first time I became aware of racism. The incident that I recount was a defining moment in my becoming aware of the effect that racism has on all of us, both people of color and whites. Racism puts a wedge between us as members of the human family and "contradicts God's will for our salvation."

In their 1979 pastoral letter, "Brothers and Sisters to Us," the United States Conference of Catholic Bishops boldly said, "racism is a sin." In the ensuing thirty years since that pastoral letter was written, racism continues to be a defining issue in our society, even as we become more aware of its insidious nature and realize that we must be proactive in addressing the sin of racism. We know that racism is not simply an individual problem; rather it is woven into the very fabric of our institutional and social structures.

I am grateful to those who have been involved in working to end the sin of racism and its effects in the institutions of the Archdiocese of Chicago, particularly the Office for Racial Justice, under the leadership of Sister Anita Baird, which spearheads this initiative. Through the Workshops on Racism and Ethnic Sensitivity and other archdiocesan anti-racism initiatives, thousands of Catholics from across the archdiocese are working to transform our institutions. However, while much has been accomplished there is still much work to be done.

The reason I began my pastoral letter on racism with my own personal story is because I believe that one of the most powerful tools that can be used to break down the walls of prejudice and racism is through the sharing of our personal stories. Our human experiences of joy and pain, challenges and triumphs are common experiences and speak to our hearts, where transformation must first begin.

The stories in this little book are both painful and inspiring to read. The witness speakers all find strength in their Catholic faith and in the enduring fortitude of their ancestors, children and grandchildren. They share their stories with the hope that future generations will be spared the pain of racism. I am deeply grateful to them for inviting us into their lives in such a personal and meaningful way. I hope that these stories of faith and endurance will be a source of inspiration for all of us as we work together to create a more racially just church and society in a civilization of love.

Let us pray that one day through the grace of God, our Father, the redeeming love of Christ, our Savior, and the power of the Holy Spirit, our Sanctifier, the world will truly be a place where people of every race, ethnicity and class will dwell together in God's infinite and universal love.

Sincerely yours in Christ,

Francis Cardinal George, OMI
Archbishop of Chicago

NOTE FROM THE EDITOR

The Archdiocese of Chicago has taken a somber look at racism as it affects the church and the surrounding community. Initially, Joseph Cardinal Bernardin and then his successor, Francis Cardinal George, gave serious direction to provide learning experiences in racism and anti-racism for people of the Archdiocese of Chicago. Francis Cardinal George wrote a pastoral entitled, "Dwell in My Love," and he initiated the Office for Racial Justice in the Archdiocese. Sr. Anita Baird, DHM, is the founding Director of the office, which began in 2000.

In addition to other tasks of the Office for Racial Justice, several types of workshops are offered for specific groups in the Archdiocese. This book contains a small sampling of the witness talks given at Workshops on Racism and Ethnic Sensitivity. At these workshops, witness speakers from various cultures present their personal experiences of racism and then reflect on how these experiences shape their lives today. I am deeply grateful to those people who were willing to share their very personal stories. I ask you, dear reader, to treat them with respect. If, in response, you wish to share your story, please do so at the website for the Office for Racial Justice of the Archdiocese of Chicago, dwellinmylove.org.

Lois Prebil, osf

PREFACE

As the "vision speaker" at many of the Workshops on Racism and Ethnic Sensitivity in the Archdiocese of Chicago, I have been privileged to see lives transformed as whites and people of color struggle with the complexities of internalized racism and prejudice in their deep desire to grow in faith and in relationship with their sisters and brothers as members of the one body of Christ.

While getting at the root cause of racism is complex, we know that racism is not inborn but rather it is carefully taught and passed on from one generation to the next. Racism has the power to damage and scar one's life, altering it forever. The personal healing of a soul scarred by the sin of internalized racism is a lifetime journey.

This very human and personal story is also a sacred one. In the workshops, thousands of people have come together from diverse backgrounds — white, black, Latino, Asian and Native American — to share their stories of race, place and grace, assured that they were in a safe environment where their stories would be heard and reverenced, a place where healing and reconciliation would begin.

As Director of the Office for Racial Justice, I am often

asked what motivates me to keep doing this work. What gives me hope? The answer is revealed in the beauty of a mural that is painted on the wall of the chapel in St. Sabina Church on the Southside of Chicago and reproduced on the cover of this book. It is by artist Samuel Akainyah and is titled, "The Last Supper to Be." Around the table are men, women and children from every tribe and nation (some famous and others not), and in the center is a very faint image of Jesus. When the mural was being painted I asked the pastor, Father Michael Pfleger, why the image of Jesus was so faint. The answer I received from Father Pfleger is what keeps me doing the work of racial justice: "Until everyone is welcome at the table, Jesus cannot come into the fullness of his glory."

Every time I enter the chapel at St. Sabina's and sit before that haunting image, I know that the work of combating racism is not in vain. I see the image of Jesus growing clearer each and every time another person is able to reclaim his or her human dignity, each and every time a story is told and a heart is changed, each and every time the walls of prejudice and racism crumble a little more, bearing witness to the truth that at the banquet of the Lord there is room for all of God's children.

Sister Anita Baird, DHM

WHAT HAPPENED THERE STILL HAUNTS ME

Yolanda Gamboa

Yolanda Gamboa is an administrative assistant at an elementary school. She works with Hispanic families and does translation of school correspondence. She feels being bilingual is a gift to be shared. Yoli is committed to being a bridge between two cultures and to working to find common ground between the diverse ethnic groups. Yoli is proud of her two teenage children. She is a Girl Scout leader and is a witness speaker at the Workshops on Racism and Ethnic Sensitivity. She believes we are all called to work for justice.

At this time I would like to share some of my thoughts on what it means to be Hispanic and how my culture has brought me joy, sorrow, pain and strength. My father came to this country over forty-eight years ago. He is from Aguascalientes Ags, Mexico. He came here to visit, met my mother, fell in love and decided to stay here and have a family. As long as I can remember, my father worked two jobs to provide us with a Catholic school education. There are five of us — four girls and one boy. We were born and raised here, but my father gifted us with the opportunity to go to Mexico every other summer to visit with our grandparents and cousins. There we learned of the rich traditions and the history of our people, of our devotion to God, the importance of faith and ritual and of the Virgin of Guadalupe. Our father taught us to take pride in who we are. He gave us the opportunity to experience what it means to be Mexican. He would sit and read with us so we could learn to read and write in Spanish. When we were young we would recite the rosary as a family during the Novena to the *Virgen de Guadalupe*. We also learned the importance of family as we ate our meals together. We felt comfortable and secure in who we were. We spoke Spanish to my father and English to my mother. My mother is of Mexican descent, but she was born here. She speaks Spanish fluently. We practiced the customs and traditions of our culture in our home.

At the age of six I didn't see myself as being much different from other children around me. I remember we had to move from our old home on West Taylor Street because the area was changing from white and Hispanic to African-American and we were getting picked on all the time. My parents knew it was time to move when a group of African-American kids pushed both my sisters and me into a large puddle of mud in an old empty lot. My parents wanted to provide us with a safe environment, so we moved into an all-white neighborhood. We were the first Mexican family on the block. I never thought of myself as different until others started telling me I was different. They would call my family "dirty Mexicans" and would tell us to go back to Mexico.

This confused me, since I was born in America and considered this country my home. We went to the Catholic school in our neighborhood. What happened there still haunts me. Not only did the children pick on us but the nuns didn't like us either. They treated us as if we were different, and I couldn't figure out why. One time during recess my class was playing a game. I wanted to play and my classmates wouldn't let me. Sister asked me why. I told her it was because they said I was a dirty Mexican. I will never forget her response, "Well, you are, aren't you?" She then made me go and sit in the classroom all by myself while everyone continued to play outside. There were several other incidents where the nuns would pick on us. One day my cousin came home from school and my aunt was so upset at what she saw. My cousin's face was bruised with fingerprints and his front

> I never thought of myself as different until others started telling me I was different.

lip was split. The sister had slapped him very hard because he didn't know an answer. My aunt could not speak English, so mother went to see the sister and told her that we had the same rights as everyone else to be there. Mother shook up sister, and that lessened the harsh treatment. But I could still tell they didn't like us. They were just less obvious after that.

So, at a young age I learned what it meant to be different. Even though I didn't feel different I was treated that way. I became a quiet child who stayed close to home. I would read a lot and spend a lot of time with my sisters. As I got older I continued to experience being seen as "Mexican." My sisters are lighter skinned than I, so they did not get picked on as much because they looked American.

After years of hard work my parents were able to purchase our first home in St. Rita of Cascia Parish. This is the Marquette Park area. This park played a big role during the Civil Rights movement. The Nazi headquarters was down the street near 67th and Western.

The mission of that community was to keep the park white. This is where Martin Luther King was struck in the head with a stone for holding a march and rally in the park. In the early 1980s, when we moved there, I decided to venture into the park. I still didn't see myself as different, yet others continued to do so. I remember the posters on park signs that had a skull and cross-bones on them saying, "Keep the Park White." One day while my sister and I were jogging in the park, she ran ahead of me because I was getting tired. Three guys on a bench barely noticed her as she ran by because of her light skin, but as I approached them they stood up and blocked my path. One asked me, "Where are your papers?" I said, "What papers?" "The ones that say you can come in this park, you S____. " I felt my blood boil. I started to walk, and they kept up with me. I said, "Oh, those kinds of papers. I thought you meant rolling papers. Those are more your style." They seemed shocked at what I said. I took off running and they yelled, "Yeah, keep running, you S____." When I reached my sister I told her what had happened. She said they didn't say a word to her. She didn't look different to them.

Through my working years I have also experienced being different. Not only am I a minority, but I am also a woman. I have found myself in a roomful of professionals who have challenged my abilities because I am a woman. I have attended many seminars in my field and have been the only Hispanic. I have not been openly welcomed into the groups that formed. I would spend a lot of time in my room. Then I realized that there is nothing wrong with me. I have the same right to be there. I know my capabilities, so I made up my mind to enter the room, greet others and ask if I might join them. Sometimes it works and other times it doesn't. But I have learned not to force the issue and try to get the best I can out of the seminars.

I am a manager of Data Services in the Telecommunications Department. I worked with an installation crew who thought I didn't know anything because I was not an installer. The joke around the group was that the only thing I could teach them was to make tortillas. So whenever some of them would see me talking with someone they would clap their hands together as if they were making tortillas. Many times people judge you by appearance. What they see externally affects how they react internally. I have two small children who are very fair. They both have very light brown hair with glints of gold in it, and my daughter has light green eyes. They look white and not Hispanic. Many times I have had people ask me if they are my children. They expect me to have children with black hair.

With experiences like these, I often wonder, "Where do I belong?" When I go to Mexico, I am seen as an American. Yet when people see me here they see me as a Mexican. I would like to share a quote from the movie "Selena." Abraham Quintanilla describes what it means to be Mexican-American. He says:

Being Mexican American is tough. Anglos jump all over you if you don't speak English perfectly.

Mexicans jump all over you if you don't speak Spanish perfectly. Our families have been here for centuries, and yet they treat us as if we just swam across the Rio Grande. We have to know about John Wayne and Pedro Infante. We've got to know about Frank Sinatra and Augustin Lara. We've got to know about Oprah and Cristina. Japanese Americans, Italian Americans, German Americans have their homelands on the other side of the ocean. Ours is right next door, and we have to prove to the Mexicans how Mexican we are and we have to prove to the Americans how American we are. We have to be more Mexican than the Mexicans and more American than the Americans, both at the same time. It's exhausting! Nobody knows how tough it is to be Mexican-American!

When I went to Mexico for a visit, I went souvenir shopping with my cousins. They told me not to open my mouth. I wondered why because I thought I spoke Spanish fluently. They said they would do the talking because the vendors would hear me speak and jack up the prices. My own cousins saw me as an American because I wasn't born in Mexico.

These are some of many experiences that have made me a stronger person. I have experienced the love of God in my life. I have learned from Jesus that we are not different. God accepts us the way we are, but at the same time expects us to become the best we can be. Then I ask the question, "If God accepts us the way we are, why can't people do this?" The dominant culture thinks their way is the best, that all should conform to their ways — that we must give up the culture and history that make us who we are. As my father did, many Hispanics continue to come here, looking for something better and living faith-filled lives with their families. They are in a strange country where many don't understand or speak the language. But they are hard workers who continue the struggle for something better. My father has won many opportunities for us, but there is much work left to be done. I carry on with the struggle.

Other experiences with racism serve as a reminder that I am still different. When my son was in kindergarten, I was at a parent-teachers meeting. I do not live in the parish, but my children attend school there because my original parish no longer has an elementary school. The teacher said my son needed to improve his motor skills. She then asked if he had a two-wheeler, to which I replied, "No, but I was going to give him one for his birthday." She then said, "Well, he probably can't ride it or play outside." I asked her what she meant. She said, "Well, you do live east of St. Louis Avenue, don't you? It is not safe over there." I then realized what she meant. Pulaski Road has been the dividing line between the whites, Hispanics and African Americans. I became angry and responded, "If my children don't play outside it is because I do not allow them to play unsupervised. When I can watch them, they play outside. Yes, the neighborhood is changing, but my children are not prisoners in our home. I am a single parent and one day when I can afford to move west of Pulaski Road, I might do that."

She responded, "Well, I guess as long as the Hispanics move in we will still be safe." I was so angry. Why did she have to bring up where I live? How she was able to determine that my son had poor motor skills — because he can't ride a two-wheeler? And he can't ride a two-wheeler because of the neighborhood in which we live? It is hard to comprehend. What else was she saying? That if the neighborhood has blacks it will no longer be safe? I shared this experience with my family. They told me I should go to the principal, but I didn't. I let it go. I knew a better way of expressing it. Little did she know that she would become a part of my talk on racism!

Several years ago, we were celebrating Girl Scout Sunday at our parish. I prepared the girls and planned the liturgy. I had started to feel accepted by the parents of the girls. But when I walked into church before the Mass started I was greeted by cold stares. As I walked up and down the aisle, I greeted those sitting in the pews. Not one person responded. I could see by their stares that they were wondering, "Who is she?" I felt my security somewhat shaken by their cold reception, but once again I reached deep inside and told myself, "You are doing fine. It will take time and there is hope." I must continue to move forward hoping their hearts will melt someday or that they can at least learn to say hello to a stranger. I truly believe there is hope. Our parish is now participating in these workshops on racism. And I was very happy to see the flyer that was distributed last Christmas. It was a bi-lingual announcement for the *Virgen De Guadalupe* celebration at the parish. The school has become very welcoming and diverse. I believe there are good people there. I have the pleasure of knowing and working with them. Good things are happening with God's help and the willingness of this faith community. A prayer at a time, one step at a time.

One final experience with racism really saddens my heart. Marquette Park has a large Arab-American population. Their businesses line 63rd Street. I have known them to be a quiet people, hard workers that keep to themselves. They have a small mosque on 63rd and Homan Avenue. The Friday after Sept. 11th, the Southwest Organizing Project organized a group of neighborhood churches to go and stand out in front of their mosque to show unity with them. At twelve o'clock noon, while they were at prayer, a human chain was formed around the front of the building. This chain was made up of a diverse group of people of different races and religions, united in a common prayer for peace, not retaliation. When our Arab friends were finished with their prayer, they came out and joined hands in prayer with the rest of us — a prayer for peace and acceptance. It was a moving and inspirational moment. Those who were there felt they had taken a stand, wanting to make a difference. But where there is prayer and unity, evil lurks near by.

> **The dominant culture thinks that we must give up the culture and history that make us who we are.**

Later that night someone broke into the mosque and destroyed it. They broke all the windows, destroyed their furniture and images and defaced the walls with senseless graffiti. It was heartbreaking. I drove past with my children and cried. I wanted them to learn from this. We are called to love one another, even when we don't always agree. I wanted them to see that evil is around. But I told them they are the future, they must work for change, but most importantly they must see beyond what a person looks like or where they come from — see who they are and what they have inside.

And that is why I share what my life experience has been and continues to be. I will not remain silent and accept the saying "That's the way it is." Once I was told, "Yoli, give it up. It's just the Hispanic's turn in the barrel. The Polish, the Irish and the Jews have all been there." My response to all of you is, "Why should anyone have a turn in the barrel?" The challenge is to change "the way it is."

> **I will not remain silent and accept the saying "That's the way it is."**

Through these experiences I have learned to celebrate who I am. My parents have given me the strength and courage to go on and, most important, to never be ashamed of who I am or where I came from. The ability to overcome adversity is nurtured by humility, patience and compassion. These are gifts I have received from my parents, gifts I will give to my children. I am blessed in many ways. I am lucky to have been born and raised here in the United States; to have the gift of speaking two languages; to discover who I am and how I can help others. How can I make a difference? I see myself as a bridge builder. I am blessed to know both cultures.

OWN THEM,
CLAIM THEM
AND NAME THEM

Sue Szarek

Sue Szarek works for a large insurance company. Sue is active with the Peace & Justice Ministry of St. Ansgar parish in Hanover Park, Illinois, and is passionate about fighting racism in all its forms. She enjoys working with the Office of Racial Justice of the Archdiocese of Chicago, and she feels very blessed and humbled to share her message. Sue's husband is a deacon in the Archdiocese of Chicago, and together they serve on various boards of their parish.

I'd like to start this by telling you about myself. I was born in a very small suburb of Buffalo, New York, named Tonawanda, a community of about 2500 people. Tonawanda was an all-white, all-Christian community. We weren't all Catholics, but we were all white Christians. There were no people of color in my church, school or neighborhood.

I remember that in my very small, very white town there was a mentally challenged boy who lived up the street. I was a few years younger than he, but I was never allowed to play with him. When I was out with my friends playing, my mom would call me into the house if he came out. It didn't occur to me at the time, but when I look back on it I believe it was because he was "different" and therefore I wasn't allowed to have him as a friend. I'd say this was my first experience with learned racism — and at this point, I didn't even know what racism was.

I didn't even know what a "person of color" was until 1969, when we moved to New Orleans for my father's job. When we arrived there, my mom made sure we moved into an all-white community. My sister and I went to a Catholic school, where there would be less chance of "those people" (as my mother called them) being there. I can remember thinking, "Who are 'those people'? Why can't I meet them?" I didn't understand what she was referring to.

I remember my first day of school. My older sister walked me to class, and when I walked in there were black children. I was terrified! I had never even seen a black person before. They must have been what Mom had been referring to. I didn't know why, but I knew I was supposed to be afraid and stay away from them. I was quickly becoming a racist. But as I began to know my new classmates, they became my friends. I couldn't understand why my mom didn't want me to become friends with "those people." Didn't everyone deserve an education? Why was she so afraid of them? Looking back on it now, I should have questioned my mother as to why she was so afraid of my new friends. But I never told her that I had made friends with people of color at school.

In 1971 we moved back to Tonawanda, to the same white neighborhood, to the same white church, and to the same white school. Only this time there was something different about my school: A Jewish girl had moved into the neighborhood. I can remember standing out in the hallway for an air raid, because we just knew that the "Commies" were going to drop a bomb on us. And there stood Sharon G____. I'll never forget her. I can still remember standing in the hallway, and she was off by herself with her head down. The rest of us all huddled together and stared at her. She "looked" like us, but she was Jewish! What was Jewish anyway? In sixth grade, my friends and I had been so protected from other races that we didn't even know. We just knew we had to stay away from her.

This was true of my entire childhood: Fear everyone who isn't a white Christian. And make jokes about them. They would never understand the jokes anyway, so they won't mind. Right? This was all I knew.

When we moved to Illinois, Mom made sure it was to an all-white community and a majority-white school. I can remember the neighborhood scandal when people of color moved in up the street. After all, people of color are all poor. Right? Aren't they all on welfare? How can they afford to live in this neighborhood?

Fast forward to about two years ago. I work for a division of a Fortune 500 insurance company. Our upper level management is predominantly white male. We have a couple of women in the high ranks, but they too are white. About two years ago, my organization hired a new vice president, who is housed in our home office in Connecticut. I had spoken with Michael over the phone several times, and didn't think much of it. He was a very nice man, who really knew what he was doing, and I was very impressed with his ideas. Then Michael came to my office in a Chicago suburb. I had set up an appointment to meet with him, and I was looking forward to talking to him face-to-face. As I walked over to the office where he was waiting, I knocked on the door and heard him say, "Come

> **Try as hard as I do, I still struggle with my racist upbringing.**

in, Sue," and I opened the door. As I did so, a black man stood up to greet me. I literally gasped. Michael looked at me and smiled and said, "Not what you expected, eh?" As I apologized and made up some excuse about how clean the office was, I remember thinking, "Why wouldn't management hire a black man? This guy clearly knows what he's doing. He has great ideas for our company, and he's probably one of the smartest men I've ever met."

When I reflect on meeting Michael, even today, I still try to understand why I was so surprised. Because he didn't sound black on the phone? Because my company historically only hired whites? Because, try as hard as I do, I still struggle with my racist upbringing? A few days later, some associates and I were talking, and in very whispered tones they asked me if I had met Michael, our new vp. I said yes, I had. "Why are we whispering?" I asked them. They responded — "Well, he's black." I looked at them and said, "He knows he's black. And just because he's black doesn't mean he's deaf."

My husband and I are currently in the Diaconate Formation Program. A couple of weeks ago, we were at an evangelization class. As we were talking about reaching people where they are, our instructor asked us what our mental picture of God is. Immediately in my mind's eye I saw an older, long-bearded man — a kind of white Santa figure. I heard a classmate of ours directly behind me, who is a person of color, say under his breath, "a white man." It struck me that I assumed a white God. And Leroy, my black friend, assumed the same thing; he didn't like it, but he did assume it. Leroy is a person of color, and he grew up with a God he couldn't relate to. He had been taught God was white.

At forty-four years of age, I've come from being afraid of a mentally challenged person who seemed different from me to giving racism workshops in my church. And here I am, listening to this man behind me, whom I've known for the last three years and have become friends with, sitting in my own shame that I "assumed" his God was white too. I fight thoughts like that every day, and I know I always will. I have to keep myself on guard and in check because of thoughts like that. But, I also know I have to own them, claim them and name them in order to change.

NO MELTING POT, BUT A DELICIOUS STEW

Joanne Kiyoko Tohei

Joanne Kiyoko Tohei is a member of the Church of Saint Ita in Chicago's racially diverse Edgewater neighborhood. Over the years she has been active in various archdiocesan organizations, but currently she concentrates her "limited energies" on speaking at workshops on racism and at ethnic sensitivity gatherings and helping in various capacities at the Office for Divine Worship. A native of San Francisco, Joanne feels deeply the importance of preserving her Japanese cultural heritage and is an enthusiastic participant in community groups that teach and perform Japanese arts such as folk music, dancing and taiko drumming.

There is a place in the State of Utah called Topaz. This name comes from a nearby mountain range, and the nickname of the place is "Jewel of the Desert." I went there over Memorial Day weekend several years ago for the first time since 1945, because I needed to make this journey. I needed to make a personal pilgrimage to the site where my family was incarcerated during World War II. After the bombing of Pearl Harbor, the American government in 1942 forced the evacuation of 120,000 people of Japanese descent from the West Coast because of wartime hysteria and the fear of espionage. And two-thirds of these people were American citizens, like myself. Those of us who were indeed citizens were never even given the courtesy of being called Americans; all those of Japanese descent were labeled either "aliens" or "non-aliens." We were all incarcerated without due process of law, behind barbed wire, in what then-President Franklin Roosevelt himself called "concentration camps." This has been described as the largest violation of individual rights by the U.S. government in the twentieth century. No charges were ever filed against us Japanese Americans; there were no trials, no due process, no justice. The sole criterion for evacuation and internment was our Japanese race and race alone.

I have always felt a deep desire to connect with this part of my past, but my family would never talk about these dark years—not only my family, but the thousands of Japanese families who to this day are reluctant to share the stories and the emotions of the incarceration experience. This silence will always remain a paradox to me. Is it a display of tremendous inner strength and resilience, or a form of denial that this criminal act resulting from racism had actually occurred in America? The void I felt could be only partially filled by the many books and historical documents I read. I needed to journey to Topaz, to walk in the dust on the actual ground of the internment camp in the barren wasteland of Utah where I spent three and a half years of my life.

When I set foot again on this desert soil, now reclaimed by sagebrush and mosquitoes, I tasted the dust and emotions washed over me as I remembered the unforgettable and confronted the unforgivable. Only by coming to pay homage to my people in Topaz to acknowledge what had happened during the war could I claim this part of history as my own and make an important connection to the past. I was too young to remember the F.B.I. coming to our house in San Francisco one night shortly after the start of the war to take my father into custody. Without charge and without trial he was sent to a federal prison, first in Bismarck, North Dakota, and then later to Lordsburg, New Mexico, simply because he ran a trucking business, unloading ships from Japan docked in San Francisco Bay and delivering their merchandise to stores in the city. Because he had contact with the enemy's vessels, this made him a suspect for espionage. It was over two years before my father was allowed to rejoin our family in Topaz, and the only reason for his release from prison was because my older brother became seriously ill and subsequently died while in camp.

I was also too young to remember that the attack on Pearl Harbor by the Japanese military was an attack against a military naval installation, not against civilians in the middle of a city (unlike the more recent September 11, 2001 incidents, which were attacks on all of America). Yet in 1942, General DeWitt, who was in charge of military operations, made the infamous remark, "A Jap is a Jap," as the government issued Executive Order 9066, stating that we Japanese Americans were to leave our homes and businesses with only those possessions we could carry ourselves.

I was also too young to remember the several months that our family spent living in a horse stall at the Tanforan Race Track outside of San Francisco. The furnishings that were provided were army cots and some sacks we had to stuff with straw ourselves so we could use them as mattresses. During the months we lived in the horse stalls, the government worked feverishly to build the various camps to which we would be sent. These camps, ten in all, were built on public land in the interior deserts, away from the West Coast, away from the population centers of America. But even these prison camps would be a welcome relief from living in horse stables, where homemade partitions between the stalls did not reach all the way up to the ceiling, so there was never any privacy; where no amount of sweeping or cleaning could clear the dirt floor of dust and wood shavings and the ever-present smell of manure. The September 11th terrorist attacks were repeatedly referred to by the media as a "second Pearl Harbor," but when we Japanese Americans hear the word "Pearl Harbor," we are painfully reminded of our mass incarceration into America's concentration camps.

After the war ended, our family was allowed to return to San Francisco to try to rebuild our lives. We were placed in a government housing project called Hunter's Point, where the cramped quarters were not too different from our barracks in Topaz.

> **In 1942, General DeWitt made the infamous remark, "A Jap is a Jap."**

We were still under a curfew; this time (according to the government) for our own safety. We had no choice, for there were unwritten rules about where in this cosmopolitan city we could rent a house. And of course, the Alien Land Law in California did not allow us to own homes or land, until the law was repealed in 1956. This was only one of the over 500 laws and statutes on the books of the State of California that discriminated against Asians during and after the war years.

While growing up, whenever I asked my parents why they would not talk about this part of our history, their response was always, "Because it was shame." It was shame for us to be forced to live in tarpaper barracks behind the barbed wire and machine gun guard towers of a concentration camp. And when I asked why there were guard towers, the answer was that this was "for our own protection." Then why were the machine guns pointed inwards towards us rather than outwards toward whatever we needed protection from? It was almost as if this racism was entirely our fault, for it never occurred to my parents and their generation to place responsibility and blame on the actions of the U.S. government. They never considered the irony of U.S. military officers visiting the camps, venturing behind barbed wire, to present posthumous awards to the parents of Japanese American soldiers — soldiers who had been killed in action overseas, fighting for the country that imprisoned their families. They never questioned the fact that we were imprisoned not because of any crime we committed but simply because of who we were.

This was the setting of my earliest memories, the environment which helped form in me a typically Japanese characteristic of trying to become invisible, to not cause any ripples. There is a saying in our

> **There were unwritten rules about where in this cosmopolitan city we could rent a house.**

culture: "The nail that sticks out will be pounded down." Therefore, we should try to go through this world without calling attention to ourselves or causing shame and embarrassment to our families, to our communities.

Was this why, when my mother enrolled me in kindergarten, she wrote the name "Joanne" on the forms? Joanne is not the name I was born with, not the name on my birth certificate and U.S. passport. Did my having an English name rather than my legal name of Kiyoko help me blend in and become invisible? Was this why, when in grammar school I used to be chased all the way home by kids calling me "Jap" and other racial slurs, I never thought about retaliating? Did I, as a young child, not feel the physical pain of the rocks they threw at me, as well as the emotional upheaval those rocks caused? The lesson in life taught by these incidents was that there are certain things that can't be helped. So why bother? Don't cause waves… Don't be the nail that sticks out to be pounded down again, to be put into the camps again… Don't allow yourself to become a target for racism again.

In high school, I had a guidance counselor who asked me what I wanted to be in life. I answered, "A secretary." (This was in the 1950s, when women still chose very traditional careers.) She asked me what school I wanted to attend, and I answered, "The University of California at Berkeley." She became almost angry as she called me "a very confused young lady." Why would I want to attend the university if I was going to be a secretary? I was unnerved but never said anything in reply… "Don't make waves; don't cause a problem." In silence, however, I thought, "Why not?" I did end up attending the University of California, and I never did become a secretary… A few years after graduation I learned that this very guidance counselor had been dismissed by the school because there were several cases of her purposely dissuading Asian students from attending institutions of higher learning: She urged them to learn a trade or to join the work force. There was still fear of "yellow peril" in the 1950s.

We Japanese children were taught by our parents that one way to gain acceptance by the larger society was to learn to excel, whether in school or in a profession. This was a way to prove ourselves. If we could not be accepted by the mainstream culture because of racist attitudes, we could still show our worthiness by being the best students, excelling in our studies, becoming the doctors and dentists and other professionals that are held in high regard by the community. We simply accepted the fact that we had to work harder to be treated equally. A by-product of this need to prove ourselves is the lingering stereotype felt not only by us Japanese but by other Asian groups as well. It is usually the Asian students in the schools who are expected to be tops in math, in science, in music. Few are known for their athletic talents or leadership skills. This "model minority" stigma only covers up prejudice.

> **This "model minority" stigma only covers up prejudice.**

My husband and I moved to Chicago in 1972 and went into a bank to open an account. The customer service person asked us what color checks did we want. Since we had no particular preference, the bank person suggested yellow, which according to him, was a good color for Japanese. I don't know how we ended up still banking there for the next several years. Was it ignorance on our part or merely resignation to a situation that we thought could not be changed?

I still bristle when I hear these kinds of racial references, and perhaps I continue to be ultra sensitive in social situations. For example, a young woman in her twenties was joking recently with other twenty-somethings and said flippantly to them, "Do you think I'm a J.A.P.?" When I turned around to face her, she elaborated, "J.A.P. means Jewish American Princess." This is still an inappropriate remark coming from this young woman, who happens to be Greek

Orthodox. This is an insult not only to me, but to our Jewish sisters as well.

One would think that the passage of time would lessen incidences of racism as people continue to come together in the United States in what is often called a "melting pot." But with the recent influx of immigrants from all over Southeast Asia, there is an increasing tendency to lump together all people of Asian descent. A couple of times while driving I have been honked at and shouted at by road ragers, "Go back to Korea where you came from" or "Where did you learn to drive — in China?"

The most disturbing incident happened several years ago at a function sponsored by the Archdiocese of Chicago. I was asked to read one of the intercessions at Mass in Tagalog, the language of the Filipino people. This seemed a sincere attempt to include all ethnic groups in the Prayers of the Faithful, but when I told the person in charge of the liturgy that I was not Filipino her response was, "Oh well, no one will know the difference!" Since this was an important gathering with the late Cardinal Bernardin in attendance, I didn't want to cause waves at the last minute and agreed to be coached in pronouncing the Tagalog petition in a pretty much phonetically accurate manner, but my heart was heavy and troubled. No one would know the difference? Do we Asians *really* all "look alike"?

We Asians — Cambodian, Thai, Korean, Filipino, Chinese, Vietnamese, Japanese, and also Indian and Pakistani among others — are as varied and different from one another as are Europeans. Germans are different from Irish. French are not the same as Bosnians or Hungarians, etc. Blacks can come from the continent of Africa or have ancestral roots in the islands of the West Indies. Those who are labeled Hispanic can be Mexican, Cuban, Puerto Rican, Chilean, Honduran, etc. No groups should be lumped together. The concept of a "melting pot" is incorrect. We do not all melt together into a gray mush. We keep our individual "lumps" separate and distinct — not as a monochromatic mush but as a wonderful stew where different foods blend together — like the meat, carrots, potatoes, peas, onions — in delicious harmony but still keeping their distinctive shapes and wonderful flavors.

REAL OR IMAGINED?

Gene Mendoza

Gene Mendoza is Senior Manager in Leadership and Organization Development for U.S. Cellular Corporation based in Chicago, Illinois. He teaches and advises managers and management teams in order to strengthen their effectiveness by living and practicing a model of values-based leadership. Gene grew up in Madrid, Spain, which afforded him a unique international experience. He is fluent in Spanish. He enjoys power yoga, playing the acoustic guitar and spending time with his family. Gene is married with two children and is a parishioner at Holy Family Community Parish in Inverness, Illinois. He holds a Bachelor of Science degree in Chemistry from the United States Naval Academy and a Master of Science degree in Organizational Development from American University. Gene is interested in promoting issues of social justice and change.

My name is Eugenio Román Mendoza. I was named after my grandfather from Monterey, México. I was honored when I was asked to talk about my personal experience on the subject of racism and ethnic sensitivity. As I thought about how racism may have impacted me personally, I must honestly admit that I surfaced more questions than answers. I stand here learning as much about the subject as you, puzzled by its complexities. Today, I want you to join me in exploring a form of racism that I call "subtle racism." Its effects are ambiguity and curiosity.

In a recent conversation with my father about this subject, he remembered something Anthony Quinn, the famous Mexican-American actor, once said in an interview — that sometimes he could not figure out if he had been discriminated against for real or if it had been in his imagination. These mental gymnastics help explain the impact of subtle racism. For example, when I lost my job ten months ago due to restructuring, I wondered for a moment whether or not discrimination may have played a role in the decision or was it only tough economics that drove the decision to eliminate my job. If any of you have ever been in this position, you know it is hard not to take it personally. I knew it was not an issue of talent or performance but rather mostly due to legitimate business circumstances; or at least that is what I told myself.

At the end of the day, however, they did not need me — a tough pill to swallow. I know of situations where companies have gone out of the way to keep this person or that person. What could I have done differently to improve my chances of staying with the company? Would it have mattered if I had been tighter with the "in-crowd"? I am the first to recognize that rational economic reasons lead companies to make the tough decisions to lay people off, but the point is that these questions crossed my mind (at the cost of emotional energy for me and my family). Have you ever wondered why top echelons of most big corporations look alike? Something behind the scenes appears to be going on that has a visible manifestation at the "top of the house," and most of these highly capable people, on the surface, do not look much like me or share my cultural background.

So, is all this for real, or is it my imagination?

Good things happen to good people, and this episode has given me the opportunity to realize a professional goal. Let me tell you a little bit about myself. I was born in Madrid, Spain, in 1963. My father is from South Texas and grew up in Mexico City. My mother is Spanish, a native of Córdoba in the region of Andalucía. They met when Dad was in the U.S. Air Force, stationed at the Torrejón Air Base in Madrid. We moved to the United States when I was a year old, and I spent my early childhood in Washington, D.C., and California. My father had promised my mother we would return to Spain after he retired from active duty, and we moved back to Madrid in 1972. I was nine years old. I attended Spanish elementary schools and later attended the Torrejón American High School. I received an appointment to the United States Naval Academy and graduated with a Bachelor of Science in Chemistry and a commission as an ensign. I served aboard two different ships and was deployed on two major cruises in the Persian Gulf and

Mediterranean respectively. After the Navy, I joined corporate America in the field of human resources. Today, I work as a leadership-development consultant, a goal I had been seeking to achieve for some time and which happened sooner than I expected.

Looking back, I do not recall having encountered racism until I returned to the United States. Even then it was not clear or blatant, because I was in a regimented environment where everyone was treated for the most part with the same rigor. If anything, I am grateful for having been given the chance to attend a prestigious institution that afforded me an invaluable world-class education.

On my induction day, however, I remember my father advising me to say that I was from Madrid when asked where I was from. Having been in the service himself, he anticipated this question would come up. Mom, on the other hand, never wanted

I do not recall having encountered racism until I returned to the United States.

me to go into the service in the first place. I said good-bye to my family, hastily found my way to my room, and stormed inside. My roommate was already there, and I introduced myself, "Hi, I'm Gene Mendoza, from Madrid, Spain!" He greeted me back with big blue wide eyes, telling me that he was from "Sioux City, Iowa!" He seemed surprised. We have since chuckled about this encounter, having realized back then they had put two people from opposite ends of the world together in the same room.

Four years later, on graduation day, while gathered with some of my friends and our families, one of my classmate's father approached my Dad with what seemed to be a condescending statement: "Your son graduated from the Naval Academy. You must be very proud." He had given the impression by the tone of his voice that I had accomplished something quite extraordinary, while also hinting that maybe somehow I didn't belong among the elite group of naval officers. There were many other parents around that day and, coincidentally or not, well intended or not, my family had been singled out for "praise." Was there something at work in this comment? (By the way, I have had a recurring dream that places me in any number of situations at the Naval Academy. In these dreams, I am inevitably always late to a parade (we had a lot of them) or I miss something, as if I am not worthy of being a part of the group. The unconscious mind is a powerful thing and dreams are often a window into it. Seemingly insignificant experiences must have added up to some kind of underlying feeling of self-doubt, but I cannot place my finger on any one event.)

Several years ago, my wife, Joellen, and I attended a class reunion at the Naval Academy. I took the opportunity to show her around, including visiting a little chapel where I used to pray. To give you a sense of the intensity of those early days at Annapolis, I would refer to God as "Sir!" in my prayers.

When we came upon the little chapel, I started to cry. Joellen hugged me and said, "This place must have been hard on you." But for the life of me, I could not figure out why I was crying.

I did have a lot of catching up to do back then as I struggled to reconcile my Spanish and American identities, dealing with torn emotions after having lived nine years of my adolescence in a completely different culture and now adapting to a new one. Just before starting my senior year at the academy, for example, I applied for and was awarded the opportunity to do a foreign exchange cruise with the Spanish Navy. It was as much a diplomatic assignment as it was a chance for me to stay connected to my beloved Spanish heritage. It was an enjoyable, special experience from which I learned a tremendous amount about myself, only to have to return to Annapolis for my final year. On top of everything the academy demanded, the double culture-shock of returning to military discipline and the American way of life made the challenge to fit in and succeed much more difficult than I had anticipated. On graduation day, I stood proud of having persevered and for what I had accomplished in four years. What part of my struggle had been real and what had been imagined?

What do you think about when you come across the name "Mendoza"? What images come to mind? My wife had an interesting experience at work. She wrote an email to a colleague for some information on a client in order to complete an assignment. He responded with, "Don't worry about it; I'll handle it." Somewhat puzzled by this, she responded with a clarification that she would be happy to do the work, that it was her job. A conversation with her boss prompted him to call this man to clarify things and to mention that she was a capable member of the team. Her partner in California subsequently called her up to explain: "I get these requests from these Mexicans on the West Coast and they mess everything up. When I saw your name, I thought you were one of them. You don't sound Mexican. I apologize." She answered. "No, I am not Mexican (she is Irish American), but I am married to a Spanish man." He did not know what to say. You might say he was "clueless." It was amazing to me to realize how a name alone could put you in a box. My wife — not I — had been affected by the stereotypes attached to our last name in the mind of one individual. It is like beginning a marathon two miles behind the official starting line. And if you run into the wrong person, you will have even more ground to cover before you get a credible chance to contribute on merit. And then you wonder if you can ever recover. Is it real or imagined?

> **Subtle racism has a way of chipping away, often unconsciously, at your sense of worth.**

Subtle racism has a way of chipping away, often unconsciously, at your sense of worth. The Arabs have often said, "The eyes are the windows to the soul." My wife and I just celebrated our sixth wedding anniversary, and I will never forget her endearing gesture of inclusion at our wedding when, standing there at the altar on a rainy afternoon in May, she looked into my eyes and said her vows to me — in Spanish. Selfless acts like this are always within our power, and they go very far in making others feel welcome and worthy. The next time you see someone "different," look into his or her eyes, feel his or her soul, and you will notice something quite familiar: a person with concerns and anxieties, with hopes and dreams, just like you and me.

I started by saying that I am learning about racism as much as you are, and I will leave you with one final phrase a memorable professor taught me in graduate school: "When in doubt do the loving thing." Be blatant about that! Thank you for caring enough to read this book.

WOUNDS THAT LEAVE DEEP SCARS

Georgina Debassige Roy

Georgina Debassige Roy is an Ojibway woman from the First Nations, Ontario, Canada. She has been married for thirty-four years and is a mother of two adult children. She is proud of her first grandson. Georgina recently earned a B.A. from Eastern Illinois University/Native American Educational Services (NAES) of Chicago. She teaches Native Ojibway language classes to the whole community at NAES College. Georgina is employed as Assistant to the Director at Anawim Center, the Native American Apostolate of the Archdiocese of Chicago, and is a member of St. Viator parish in Chicago. Her heart and soul are with the Anawim people. She is studying for a master's degree in pastoral studies at Catholic Theological Union. Georgina says this is "not bad for a 'country girl' who was not privileged to experience equal education."

I once saw my mother being watched and treated like a thief. We were in a store that had everything from foods to tools, the one and only store for a hundred miles. The storekeeper motioned for the saleslady to follow us very closely. My mother began to shop — touching, smelling and admiring fabric that she was going to purchase. She planned to make new clothing for the whole family. She was a great seamstress in her early years. But the clerk disinfected whatever my mother had touched; I watched as the saleslady wiped off any imprint that my mother might have left on the material. She shook each piece of fabric as if my mother had fleas. I also saw this same saleslady greet non-native people with smiles and ask if they needed help. She never asked us. Did I mention we are Ojibways? That day I knew there was something different about our skin. I was only eight years old.

I was privileged to grow up in a Native traditional home. I am Ojibway. My parents taught us all the things we need in life. But the Canadian government said it's the law that we must attend public school or residential school. In my early childhood I experienced racism several times. I was told by most of my teachers that because of my heritage I would never amount to anything or ever leave the reservation.

I experienced verbal abuse and also physical and emotional abuse in grade school, the effects of which lasted well into my adult life. In Canada, schoolteachers and religious leaders punished me wickedly, along with my Native classmates. We were forbidden to speak the Ojibway language on school property. My mother confronted these teachers for abusing us, using her own words in the Ojibway language, but she did not prevail. They yelled at her to "Speak English only; we don't understand you; there are no translators to help you; go home." Most Native parents were forcibly removed from school property for advocating for their children. It took many years and many good souls to persuade me that I was gifted and had self worth to undo what had been suppressed in me

It took many years and many good souls to persuade me that I was gifted and had self worth.

by my abusers. The taunted memories replayed over and over in my head, devaluing my child-spirit and bruising me for a long while. Those were my impressionable years.

I always knew I would be in some kind of religious field as an adult. In seventh grade, on career day, I announced out loud that I wanted to be a nun. I was told by my catechism teacher, who was a nun, that I was not worthy and they "did not accept savages as nuns." She said, "You would make a great bump on a log. Next person."

I remember another incident. We were being coached by Sister before going to confession. I was eleven as I entered the confessional saying, "Bless me Father for I have sinned; it has been one week since my last confession. Father, today I have no sins." He nearly jumped out of his chair and said, "You did not think bad thoughts? Or say evil things about your teachers? Or touch your private place? Ask forgiveness for being born Indian!" I did not understand what he meant by his questions. "Your penance is ten Hail Marys, three Our Fathers, one Act of Contrition. Now go!"

I went back to the pew and knelt and prayed my penance. I heard snickers behind me in church. Some of my classmates were making fun of me because I was kneeling too long. They said I must have done something wicked and was being punished by God. I could not discuss this with anyone without committing another sin, however, because of the seal of confession.

My son's first week in kindergarten is one I remember. It was 1979. My cousin, Levina, and I stood looking blankly at each other afterwards because of what my son's teacher said in our presence. I was having a conversation with her about my son not knowing the Pledge of Allegiance and having problems tying his shoes. In the meantime, the other children in the classroom were acting out. She yelled out at them, "Children stop acting like a bunch of wild Indians," in front of me. I just swallowed another mouthful of racial remarks that day. On our way home I said, "I will not let this ugliness happen to me again."

As an adult I heard God's call to me to be his servant. I was praying, asking God to reveal my gifts to me, and to put me in a place I could use my Ojibway language. I answered God's call and I volunteered for seventeen years among my Native American Indian community. I grew in confidence after attending Called and Gifted, the two-year lay ministry program offered by the Archdiocese of Chicago. I did my two-year practicum at the Anawim Center/Native American Apostolate and was hired in 2001 as the Assistant to the Director.

My people have dealt with many generations of painful attacks, insults and harsh words about our race. We have wounds that have left deep scars from those in the dominant culture. Sometimes I feel my people are treated just like Our Lord Jesus Christ, who was tortured to death.

WE WEAR THE MASK

Patricia Anderson

Patricia Anderson is proud to say that she is a "cradle Catholic." Patricia, her mother who lives with her, and her grandmother all graduated from Holy Ghost Catholic School in Jackson, Mississippi. She is now a Spanish teacher at Walter H. Dyett High School in Chicago. She belongs to Holy Angels Catholic Church, where she is enthusiastically involved in church organizations and events. Patricia continues to be active in WRES, Workshops on Racism and Ethnic Sensitivity in the Archdiocese of Chicago. As part of WRES she reaches out to other churches to raise awareness that racism still exists. She wears, as she says, "many hats."

I call my witness to racism talk, "We Wear the Mask," referring to a poem written in the late nineteenth or early twentieth century by Paul Lawrence Dunbar. You know, this mask is still being worn one hundred years later for many of the same reasons!

I was born and grew up in Jackson, Mississippi. The first encounter with racism and prejudice that I vividly remember was with two little girls who happened to be white and were my neighbors. This was in the early 1950s. We played together for about four years, every day except on Sundays. They went to their church and I went to mine. Guess what? We were all Catholic! After finishing my homework or Saturday chores I would usually go outside to jump rope, laugh and talk with my friends. I was only eight years old. One day I called for them to come on over and the older one ran to the fence and whispered, "We can't play with you anymore." The younger one blurted out, "Because you're a n_____!" This undoubtedly had a great impact on me, because I have never forgotten it. However, life goes on. I forget just why!

I went on to finish grade school and high school and entered Jackson State College as a freshman in the summer of 1961. Off-campus meetings, marches, sit-ins, demonstrations, freedom riders, etc., were many. Twelve years of Catholic schooling did not prepare me for so much racism, because I had been taught that I could do whatever I chose to do and color never entered the picture. But, oh, how different things were as I entered the outside world as an eighteen-year-old!

James Meredith, a former student at Jackson State, integrated the University of Mississippi ("Ole Miss") in 1963. After the governor stated that there would be no "Nigras" admitted to Ole Miss, Robert Kennedy, then Attorney General, sent the National Guard to Oxford, Mississippi. Violence destroyed many buildings on the campus. However, Meredith eventually became a full-time student during his senior year and was the first Negro to graduate from the University of Mississippi.

In 1965, my senior year at Jackson State, I began applying to graduate schools all over the U.S. I applied to Ole Miss simply because I wanted to know what was there that some white people did not want me to see. The courts had placed eight other Negro students there, but I did not go through the courts. I received an acceptance letter on my own accord, and of course I went there!

This turned out to be probably the worst year of my whole life. When I arrived at Ole Miss with my family, the first thing I heard when I got out of the station wagon was, "What? Another n_____?" I was placed in the graduate dorm and, of course, was the only Negro there! My room was just across the hall from the bathroom. Was it for my convenience or for what exactly? I'll never know.

On my first night there, girls, certainly not ladies, ran up and down the halls yelling loudly, "I'm not going to shower in the same bathroom with a n_____." "I'm not going to use the same toilet as a n_____!"

> **I had been taught that I could do whatever I chose to do and color never entered the picture.**

I laughed at them because we, as a people, have a saying, "Sticks and stones may break my bones, but words will never hurt me!" I used that saying to build a wall around myself, so that no matter what was said to me, I would never break.

I was baptized when I was two weeks old, brought up in a Catholic home, went to Catholic school for twelve years, and taught that I could always go into a Catholic church to pray. So I found the one Catholic church in Jackson and went to Mass that Sunday morning. Wow! The mean stares that I got that morning! So mean that I was actually afraid to go to Communion because these people seemed ready to kill me, if at all possible.

I went to class on my first Monday there, and the professor with a deep southern accent called roll. I got in trouble immediately because I laughed as he called my name, "Señorita Patricia Anderson." I did not go to class on the next day. A fellow student came by my dorm and suggested that I drop the class. Of course I asked why. He told me that when the professor called my name that morning, he stated that he hates Catholics, "Nigras" and Jews and that "Señorita Anderson" has two strikes against her.

Remember my wall? I went to the teacher's office, explained that I would drop his class if he would give me a WP (withdrawal pass) as opposed to a WF (withdrawal failure). I told him, "If you fail me, I will take you to court!" He gave me a WP. Later that school year, I received a phone call from the Experiment in International Living concerning a scholarship. Thinking it was a prank call, I hung up. The man called right back, and I told him that I did not have time for joking. He said, "Just listen, Ms. Anderson. You have received one of seven Sargent Shriver scholarships given in the United States. I will send you all of the necessary papers immediately." The next morning I went to breakfast in the cafeteria and a young lady walked over and threw an article on my table. It was torn out of a newspaper, and it read, "Ole Miss Negro Student Wins Scholarship to Peru." I turned to thank her, but she was gone.

That afternoon I went to dinner and a teacher came to my table and said "Congratulations, but you still will get only a 'C' in my class because I don't think you deserve a high grade." Of course he did not finish his sentence with "because you are a n____," but I knew what he wanted to say. This was the English class that I had picked up after dropping the Spanish class. I learned no Spanish, French, or English that year at Ole Miss, only how to get along with other cultures and how to survive in a hateful society. All that I have told you about and more is why I also love this poem, "We Wear the Mask":

> We wear the mask that grins and lies,
> It hides our cheeks and shades our eyes —
> This debt we pay to human guile;
> With torn and bleeding hearts we smile,
> And mouth with myriad subtleties.
>
> Why should the world be over-wise,
> In counting all our tears and sighs?
> Nay, let them only see us, while
> We wear the mask.
>
> We smile, but, O great Christ, our cries
> To thee from tortured souls arise.
> We sing, but oh the clay is vile
> Beneath our feet, and long the mile;
> But let the world dream otherwise,
> We wear the mask!

("We Wear the Mask" is from *The Complete Poems of Paul Lawrence Dunbar* by Paul Lawrence Dunbar, New York: Dodd, Mead, and Co., 1913.)

I LOVE WHO I AM

Lupe Rynkiewicz

Lupe Rynkiewicz is very active in her parish, Most Blessed Trininty, in Waukegan, Illinois, along with her husband, who is a permanent deacon. They have been happily married for the last nineteen years. She is retired from Abbott Laboratories. Lupe received her Pastoral Ministry Certificate from the University of Saint Mary of the Lake, having participated in the Deacon Formation Program. She has also enjoyed taking classes at the College of Lake County in courses such as photography, creative writing and social studies. Lupe has two children and a stepson. Her three grandsons and granddaughter are the joy of her life. She travels often to Florida where her son and his family live.

Hola, me llamo Lupe. Soy Mexicana. Neci Lupe Esparza, en Houston, Texas. Nunca me quiera a yo mismo. Yo quiere ser blanca. Hello, my name is Lupe; I am Mexican. I was born Lupe Esparza, in Houston, Texas. I never liked who I was. I always wanted to be white.

And so I will begin my story with the internalizing self-talk I used to have that no one else could hear.

I come from a hardworking religious Mexican family of seven. Nine, including my mom and dad. I had two older sisters and two younger ones; I have one older brother and one younger. I guess you could call me the middle child. My mom and dad moved us from Houston when I was around five years old. He had heard there was work, as well as farmland, in Illinois.

We lived on Market Street in Waukegan. That is where all the Mexicans lived — down by the railroad track. We had a small upstairs apartment. There were "only" seven of us then. My dad did not like us living on Market Street. He did not like the crowded Mexican neighborhood. He wanted better for us. Market Street was just not good enough for him. He wanted land to plant corn and tomatoes and to have chickens and cows. So Dad built our new home on Wadsworth Road and we left our Mexican friends behind. To tell the truth, Dad liked to talk as if he were much better than they were.

I started first grade at Howe School. It was about the third grade when I began to dislike my name very much. It happened during the exchange of valentines; everyone would spell my name wrong, and I felt they were making fun of it. Maybe they just liked to say it. They would spell my name "Loopy," "Lupee," "Loupe." I asked my mom why she didn't name me Jane or Barb or Nancy. I wanted to have a name like the rest of the girls in my classroom. I wanted to be like them. They were all white girls, and I was the one Mexican girl in class. I disliked myself for not being like them. I was quiet and shy. I talked with them but felt I was not like them. As the only Mexican girl in class, different from the rest, I thought of myself

> As the only Mexican girl in class, different from the rest, I thought of myself as having something wrong with me.

as having something wrong with me.

Well, you have a special name, my mom would say; you are named "Lupe" after our *Virgen de Guadalupe*.

It did not make me feel special. I didn't even know who the *Virgen* is; her name made me feel different from the rest. It made me wish for a normal name. I did not consider "Lupe" normal.

I was young and did not know how much damage and hurt I was doing to myself. I believe the kids liked me; they did nothing wrong to me; they played with me. In fact, they wanted to be with me. Even the little boys chased me. I just considered myself inferior to them. Not like them. How I longed to be white!

I learned my English and writing very well. I did not speak Spanish at home the way my mom and dad did. I spoke English. Oh, I understood every word they said to me in Spanish. I just did not want to speak

Spanish; I did not like it. It was different from the way the kids talked in school. I wanted to be like them. But how could I be like them? I was "I," but I did not want to accept that. It was a constant thing on my mind. Why can't I be like them?

During the summer months after the school year was out, my mom and dad would take all us kids to work out in the fields. We picked onions mostly. The owner gave us ten cents a hamper. We were good; the owner would say we were his best family. I never saw any of the money, of course; it went towards our school supplies and clothes. I was good at picking; I loved the feel of the soil and the smell of those sweet onions. I also loved pleasing my parents, so I wanted to do well and fill many hampers.

However, what I loved the most was breaks and lunch. We had fun, all of us fighting for a pop and those delicious flour tortillas Mom would fill with her potatoes and beans. I treasure those memories; it was a time most people will never understand or get to enjoy. Working out in the fields taught me to be a hard worker, to give it my best to help the family.

At that time though, I would not dare tell any of my white friends what we did all day. I was ashamed of telling them; yet I enjoyed it. When asked about how I spent my summer, I would just say, "Playing," which was not really a lie. I would hear about their vacations and how they went to the beach or visited their grandparents. I wish I could have gone to the beach like the white girls.

One day, years ago, I am getting on the school bus; it is around the time I am in eighth grade. I am happy today because today I am wearing a new outfit. Well, it is not really a "new" outfit; my mom had gotten it for me at a rummage sale. But I love it. It is a beautiful red skirt with tiny pretty flowers on it; the material is lightly padded and it is full, very full, full enough for me to put a petticoat under it. And one more thing — it has a poodle on it. The poodle has a leash around its neck and the leash goes half way around the skirt. The poodle is white and has a bow in its hair. I am so proud! I have on a white blouse that matches the skirt. It has tiny red flowers around the collar. I have on white and black saddle shoes with white socks. I am so full of joy! And my hair. It is in a ponytail. I look and feel like someone on the Dick Clark's American Bandstand show.

Anyway, I get on the bus and sit next to Janet. She is a very pretty, popular white girl, and I sit next to her when she smiles at me. Even though I do not feel good enough to be with her most of the time, this particular day I did. As Janet is looking at my outfit, she says, "I had a skirt like that; my mom gave it away — it was my favorite skirt." She continues looking at it and finally says, "Why, that *is* my skirt." I was silent for a moment, and then I said, "I don't know, my mom got this for me." Janet just keeps looking at me and my outfit. I say quietly, "I really love it." I was so embarrassed and ashamed. I think she must have felt sorry for me because we had to buy used clothes. My joy was stripped and I began hating who I was — "a poor Mexican girl." I am supposed to be better than that. My father lied. I am no better.

That was when I really started to dislike and deny who I was. I learned English very well, denying my Spanish. I only wanted new clothes from then on. My mom labeled me as the "rich one" in the family. My presents had to come from expensive stores. I did not want to share anything about my home life with anyone. I began acting like my white friends. I combed my hair as they did, and I dressed like them.

On the other hand, I loved being religious and having my mom making my pretty Easter dresses. I loved the pile of tortillas and beans that she would make. I loved who I was when I was with my family, but I denied it all when I was with the white girls. During those years I would hear things from my parents like "you're just as good as *them*"; "dress nice so *they* will be jealous"; "show off, let *them* be envious of *you*."

I guess that made me not okay with who I am. Was it better to be white than Mexican?

One more thing: my dad said to "never marry a guy from Mexico, he either has nothing or he already has a wife and kids and is up here working." I was very confused. Should I be white? Is that who I am?

It was quite difficult for me to go back to the past and see just how much damage I have done to myself. It does make me cry for the special unique person I should have been.

My dad was a racist. He talked about the blacks, we're better; he talked about the Mexicans from Mexico, we're better; he talked about the white people, and I interpreted that as his wanting me to be white.

It has taken me years to forgive him for all the damage he did to me, but now I miss him and love him tremendously. It was because I loved him so much that I believed every word he said. I trusted him to know what was good for me.

I honestly believe my dad meant no harm. He wanted the best for me; he wanted me to fit in, to get ahead in society. Nothing wrong with that. The only

I was pushing down all the things I should have been accepting about myself.

wrong thing was denying who I am; I was pushing down all the things I should have been accepting about myself.

My first husband was like my dad, so my non-acceptance of who I am continued into adult life. However, for the last eighteen years my husband, Steve, has embraced who I am, He has educated me on the *Virgen de Guadalupe*; he is learning Spanish; he loves the Mexican food that I cook and has taken me to Mexico to visit my roots. He is white, and I am an educated, beautiful Mexican woman, learning more and more each day how to be exactly that!

My name is Lupe. I am Mexican and I love who I am.

THE SCARS HAVE A DEEP EFFECT

Frances Chikahisa

Frances Chikahisa is a licensed clinical social worker who has a private practice in Chicago. In that capacity she works with senior citizens at the Japanese American Service Committee. She is a member of St. Clement parish and was active with their racial justice committee for several years. At present she is helping to establish a program for seniors in the parish. She is an active member of the Japanese American Citizens' League, a national civil rights organization. After her husband's death ten years ago, Frances moved to Chicago to be near her married daughter. She has since become the grandmother to a grandson and a granddaughter. Frances also has a son who moved to Chicago within the past five years.

My story about my experience in America's concentration camps during World War Two is one that I feel an urgency to tell over and over. After the events of September 11, 2001 and with the on-going pursuit of Al Qaeda terrorists and the subsequent arrest and detainment of many persons suspected of terror, my story has deeper implications for all Americans. Additionally, the current scandal in the Church is cause for us to ponder the long-standing consequences of relationships that do not honor another person's dignity.

December 7, 1941. It is a sunny California Sunday morning and I am attending Mass at the Japanese Catholic Mission School in Los Angeles. It is during the Mass that Father Lavery solemnly announces that Japan had bombed Pearl Harbor that morning and that we were at war. Mass is hastily concluded, and I remember feeling numb, frightened, hoping against hope that it was a bad dream.

I was almost thirteen years of age, in the eighth grade of this Catholic Mission School, a school dedicated to educating children of Japanese immigrants, 99% of whom were non-Catholics, including me. All of us were American-born children of a large Japanese immigrant population that lived in the heart of Los Angeles. While the rest of the country was swept up in a frenzy of patriotism, our community began a long and dark wartime journey that has left deep scars upon each and every one of us.

I am a survivor of the American concentration camps that housed almost all of the Japanese Americans who lived in the U.S. at the outset of WWII. About 120,000 of us were incarcerated in prisons for three to three and a half years. We were imprisoned without trial, without a hearing, without even being charged with specific acts of treason. We were ordered into camps by executive order, signed by President Roosevelt. This was done under the presumption that we were espionage risks, even if there was never one such documented case. This is a proven fact! Furthermore, the order was carried out by the military — armed soldiers who

> **While the rest of the country was swept up in a frenzy of patriotism, our community began a long and dark wartime journey.**

took over our lives, simply because we were Japanese and the country was at war with Japan. Two-thirds of us were children and, even more devastating, all the children were citizens of the U.S.

All of the immigrant parents were legal aliens who were forbidden by law to ever become naturalized citizens. Most of you probably know the history of the prejudice and racism that the Asians encountered on the West Coast in the early part of the twentieth century. I believe, however, that the rest of the country must have held these same attitudes. Otherwise, wouldn't there have been a public outcry against what was done to us?

When our parents entered this country, they were not allowed to become citizens. The interpretation of the U.S. Constitution was that citizenship was permitted to whites and freed slaves. Since Asians were neither white nor black, it was decided that we were ineligible. Inter-racial marriages were also not allowed, particularly on the West Coast, but these laws also existed in other parts of the country. Our parents were not permitted to purchase land. In every way, the Japanese immigrants lived in a climate of defined racism, without hope of ever finding the equality guaranteed by our Constitution.

The priests, nuns and brothers of the Maryknoll community who operated this mission were the only Caucasians I knew. I was living in a neighborhood that had become primarily African-American. Again, minorities were relegated to living in less desirable neighborhoods by the practice of restrictive covenants.

As we were herded into the camps, beginning in April 1942, our first "new home," called an "assembly center," was in the parking lot of a horseracing stadium. The early internees were housed in the actual horse stalls. In fact, as many as five members of one family were housed in one stall! My family, however, was fortunate. We were assigned to one of the new barracks, which consisted of one room with no running water, no toilets, and a single glaring bulb for electricity. We shared the barrack with five other families. My stoic and long-suffering parents would not allow us to complain. They kept reminding us that everyone was suffering the same indignities and humiliation.

My father, who had a successful business and took great pride in being able to take care of his family, endured the dismantling of his business, losing everything that he had spent thirty years establishing. Most of all, he suffered loss of control and the ability to protect his family. We choked down the humiliation we felt in using communal latrines and showers. There weren't even doors or curtains. Meals were served in large mess halls, with a gong sounding the call to meals. Laundry was done in communal areas. We learned to stand in long lines for everything.

Looming above the barracks was the racetrack grandstand, where we were permitted the use of the lobbies to offer community activities and classes.

Sunday Mass was offered there. Imagine Mass being offered with the betting windows as a backdrop! Outside in the stands hung huge nets, which were laced with burlap strips as camouflage nets to be used by the Army. Some of the older inmates worked on those, earning a grand sum of thirteen dollars a month. We couldn't be trusted as citizens, but our labor was acceptable for the war effort.

Most humiliating was the barbed wire fencing enclosing the whole compound, guarded by military police, with their guns pointed inward. At night the entire camp was lit up by searchlights, continually panning the area with broad beams of light.

My parents watched in horror as my older sister underwent surgery for a ruptured appendix. The surgery was performed in the former veterinary hospital, now converted for human use. She nearly died that night but held on, only to develop a secondary illness — tuberculosis. This meant that she had to be removed to a county facility because of the public health risk. We had no phones and certainly no passes out of our prison, so we were never able to talk to or visit with my sister after she was placed in the sanitarium.

Several months later our family was ordered into the more permanent interior camps — our destination was the southeast corner of Arkansas. For the first time our family was separated, not knowing if and when we would get back together. Can you imagine an indeterminate prison sentence? Not only were we in prison without charges, we were incarcerated for an undetermined prison sentence.

By the time we moved inland, we had become accustomed to being ordered like sheep. We were really getting numb to all the indignities and humiliations. No one ever talked about it. In fact, the community censored those who spoke out

> **We couldn't be trusted as citizens, but our labor was acceptable for the war effort.**

negatively. It turned out to be our patriotic duty to not complain—to show our strength by enduring.

My new school was staffed by an odd mixture of teachers hastily brought together: some were transfers from the Bureau of Indian Affairs (by and large the poorest teachers), some were American Friends who were conscientious objectors and who were generally the best instructors, others were part-time missionaries, and a few were Japanese American inmates. Supplies were meager, equipment old and outdated, and the classes were conducted in barracks, the same type that housed us. When it was hot, we sweltered; in the cold we shivered or got overheated, depending on the proximity of our seat to the stove. Mostly it rained and got muddy and we tramped from classroom to classroom. In spite of all these disadvantages, our high school was soon ranked among the highest in Arkansas.

I spent three of my four high school years in Arkansas, only once leaving the camp to attend a Y camp in Mississippi. Six of us were selected to attend this conference, and I had my first experience in the South with segregation. When we boarded the bus, there was no room for us, but we were given seats in front of the black section and the blacks were made to move back, even when there were no seats for them. In Los Angeles I had lived in a largely African-American neighborhood and had wanted very much to talk to our neighbors, but their eyes were always averted and they looked hostile. I had the same experience on this bus.

A Maryknoll priest was also assigned to our camp. He was an Irish American who had been in Japan and was imprisoned there for a short while before coming to attend to our spiritual needs. I recall having a discussion with him about segregation, and I still remember his remark that the blacks were better off with a separate but "equal" social system. His response was ludicrous to me, and it was my first experience with prejudice within the Church. The fact that I was imprisoned as a result of racial prejudice seemed to him to be totally unconnected to the plight of the African American.

Although I was not baptized as a Catholic, I had attended Mass since kindergarten, and during the war years the priests who came to camp were the only non-Japanese friends we had. This loyalty impressed my family and me and remained our thread of contact with the outside world. It became the motivating factor for all of us to embrace the Catholic faith after our return to our former life.

In the last year of incarceration, my younger sister contracted pleurisy, culminating in tuberculosis also. I can still feel how heavily my mother carried this burden. She never gave in to the feelings of depression that I'm certain she felt. I have always admired my parents' resolve to maintain pride and control over themselves and their family in spite of all these destructive events. They insisted that I visit my sister regularly at the hospital, reminding me firmly that I still had some physical freedom. Furthermore, as soon as it became possible, my parents would bring our dinner meals from the mess hall and we would eat together in the barracks rather than in the communal dining area. It was their attempt to preserve our family. Even from my teenage viewpoint, I could see that parental authority was seriously damaged. Most of the children preferred to eat with their own peer groups, hang out with their friends, and were getting beyond the control of their parents.

By this time, some of the families were moving out of camp. But relocating to another state was never an option for us since both my sisters were ill. We also had a home in California, so we hoped for the day when we could return. That day arrived in May of 1945 when we boarded a train for the return trip, my younger sister still bed-ridden, returning to the state where my older sister was awaiting discharge. Although we were back in California, my younger sister was still out of our home, in a tuberculosis sanatorium.

Putting our lives back together had its difficulties — I had grown into a raging teenager and my older sister couldn't handle the change in me. She had spent three years in a hospital bed and felt she had missed out on something, even if it was camp life in Arkansas. My younger sister was bedridden, missing several years of high school, and her return to normal life was put on hold. My parents had the difficult task of holding us all together as a family in spite of the fact that we weren't physically together yet. Furthermore, my father was in a quandary about how to earn a livelihood. It was the first time I had ever observed him immobilized as he drifted around trying to decide how to earn a living. He saw starting up a business as too risky. He had depleted much of his savings during those camp years. He finally settled on becoming a gardener — after years of managing a business he was now going to return to being a laborer. I was both relieved and ashamed — relieved that he was going to work, ashamed that he was going to do such lowly work. I was now in

college, attending UCLA and ashamed that he could not provide us with more amenities. It was the first time in my life that I felt we were poor.

This was a period of great tension. In spite of the fact that we had a home, furnishings and a car, our family life had been so fragmented that we were having great difficulty coming together. Within a year or so, my younger sister returned home, but she and I found ourselves very disconnected from each other. None of us talked about these issues but plodded ahead, as this was the culturally appropriate thing to do. My parents' insistence that we remain a family was the single source of strength that carried us through those difficult times.

All of us suffered from a deep and abiding sense of humiliation and shame. We repressed it so successfully that it's taken me fifty years to begin to acknowledge these feelings. It has been said that

> **My parents' insistence that we remain a family was the single source of strength that carried us through those difficult times.**

the camps were for our protection from an angered populace. If that were true, why were the guards always pointing their guns inward toward us? If there were actual traitors among us, why were not the rest of us released as soon as they were discovered? As I said earlier, the government files have clearly documented that there never was a case of espionage among us. The scars from the sense of humiliation and shame have had a deep effect on me, and only by talking about the past have I been able to achieve some healing.

GOING OUT OF OUR COMFORT ZONES

Joe Hanafee

Joe Hanafee is a member of St. Raymond de Penafort parish in Mt. Prospect, Illinois. He has been a member of the WRES (Workshops and Racism and Ethnic Sensitivity) team since attending the first workshop organized by his cluster in October of 2001. Dealing with issues of racism and ethnic sensitivity has been a lifelong passion for Joe. He serves as the Coordinator of the Racial and Ethnic Sensitivity Ministry at St. Raymond's and is also a lector and a member of the parish council. He and his wife, Liz, have two children, eight and five years old. Joe is their primary caregiver. He is also a part-time academic advisor at Oakton Community College.

I grew up in the city of Detroit. When I was eight years old, the 1967 riots occurred there. The center of the riots was on Twelfth Street, less than five miles from my house. My neighborhood was then 95% white. By the time I graduated from high school in 1977, the neighborhood was 70% black. White flight was quick and rapid. Many of my friends moved to the suburbs and tensions were sometimes high between the races. I often heard racial slurs from my friends and their families, and I had several experiences that could have turned me into a bigot.

I remember one experience in particular. I was walking home with two white friends from my Jesuit High School on a major street in my neighborhood called Livernois. We often referred to it as "N_ _ _ _ _ nois." The local public elementary school had just let out, and a large group of black students was walking towards us in the opposite direction. They did not move to the side as we passed. There was no place for us to walk, and some of them bumped into us. A pushing and shoving melee ensued, and I ended up running into the middle of the seven-lane street. One of my friends had also gotten away, but one was still on the sidewalk, surrounded by the black students. A white man pulled up in a car and asked me if we needed any help. I saw a gun on the passenger seat of his car. Luckily, at that moment, the "Red Sea" of black kids parted and my friend walked out of the crowd. The thing that scared me the most about this incident was seeing the gun, because I figured things were about to escalate. I don't remember afterwards having strong prejudicial sentiments toward the black students, but I do remember how scared I was by the white man with a gun.

I attribute some of my attitudes towards race to the example set by my parents. I think that their example is one of the reasons I did not have the prevalent negative stereotypes of African Americans that many of my friends had. Any I did have were balanced by positive experiences, perceptions and attitudes. My parents did not leave the neighborhood.

> I don't remember afterwards having strong prejudicial sentiments toward the black students, but I do remember how scared I was by the white man with a gun.

Mom still lives there, and the neighborhood is now 80-90% black. Dad and Mom always taught us to respect everyone, and they never made prejudicial remarks.

For many years, I wore the fact that we did not leave the neighborhood as a "badge of honor" — that we had stayed when most of the whites had left. My family had taken a stand, and I was proud of it. Ironically, when I asked my Mom about this many years later she said that she had wanted to move. She said the only reason we didn't move was because Dad set a limit on what she could spend on a new house — a limit she thinks was set purposefully low by Dad, knowing she wouldn't be able to find anything for that price. So perhaps the real reason we didn't move was that my dad was cheap (and maybe a little bit sneaky).

A defining moment in my attitudes toward

racial relations occurred when my high school went through a discernment process about whether the school should leave the city and move to the suburbs. Almost all the other Catholic high schools were either closing or moving to the suburbs. Our student body was somewhat diverse, approximately 1/3 black and 2/3 white, but enrollment was dropping and the neighborhood around the school was almost 90% black. White people were afraid to send their children there. I was convinced that the only thing that would save the school was to move it to the suburbs. What was happening was unfortunate, I thought, but you couldn't fight it. It was the safe thing to do, or so the conventional wisdom went.

In an unpopular decision, the Jesuits decided to stay. The school went through some lean years but eventually reversed course. It is now thriving. That taught me a lesson — that making the tough decision, the unpopular decision, but the right decision is what we are called, as Christians, to do.

As an adult, I have tried to follow that lesson by living in diverse neighborhoods, even when the conventional wisdom was that they weren't safe. I have never had a problem and have learned that living in diverse neighborhoods can be safe, even if I am sometimes uncomfortable. I believe that this has made me a more tolerant, accepting and loving person.

I close with something I heard shortly after 9/11; it was a reflection on a quote by the famous Lutheran theologian Dietrich Bonhoeffer. He said that most people think of peace and security as synonyms. In fact, he said, there is no peace if people always do the safe, secure thing. In order for peace to occur between people, we must go out of our comfort zones and embrace the differences among us. I think this is especially true as we look at racial relations in our country: If we want to live in peace, we cannot let safety and security be our defining values. We must go out of our comfort zones.

GET IT RIGHT

Deacon Dexter Watson

Deacon Dexter G. Watson is a native of the West Side of Chicago. He is a permanent deacon for the Archdiocese of Chicago and ministers at Holy Angels and St. Malachy parishes in Chicago. In the past he served as the alderman of the Twenty-Seventh Ward. Dexter is also a community activist and a business entrepreneur. He has received a number of honors and awards, including the Augustus Tolton Award, Alderman of the Year Award, Greenpeace Award and Parent of the Decade Award. God and his family are first in his life. Dexter's greatest treasures are Robin, his wife of twenty-nine years, and his three young-adult children, Dexter Gary II, Amber Joi and Ryan Blake.

I was born in Chicago, Illinois, on November 17, 1951. I am a black man born in America. I am a black American. As a young person of the civil rights era, I was certain blacks contributed greatly to this country, but I wanted to know the details. In 1969, as seniors in high school, my classmates and I chose to boycott our classes in an effort to fight to have black history taught to us in school. We risked expulsion from school only months before graduation. To this day, I appreciate the father of one my classmates standing up for us. He asked the principal and administration to figure out a way where we could get taught black history and stay in school. Happily, our history teacher convinced the authorities that he could switch the curriculum from ancient history to black history. Their courage saved us, and our persistence helped reshape our world. My whole life could have been changed because of this incident.

A year or two later I was driving north on Rush Street on Chicago's near north side when I thought I heard, "Hey, n_____." I immediately stopped my car in the middle of the street, left my car running, got out and went over to confront the person. He was a young, white man. I asked him if he had said what

I thought I had heard. He was a little hesitant, but claimed he had not said that. I returned to my car and drove off. I reflect on that incident today and realize my whole life could have changed if something different had transpired. My car could have been stolen. The police could have arrested me and escorted me to jail. I could have developed a record — and become another statistic. I could have gotten violent. I could have been shot or beaten up. My whole life could have been changed because of this incident.

A few years after this my Catholic grammar school was closed. This caused me to leave the Catholic Church. I felt deserted. I felt my community and I had been raped and abused. As a result, I decided to join a different church. I searched churches far and wide, left and right — Pentecostal, Lutheran, Baptist were a few. Although I had been baptized Catholic when I was in first grade, I made a point to get baptized at each church I attended. However, I never felt welcomed at any of them. I returned to the Catholic Church when I saw that a black priest had adopted a couple of black boys. He spoke in a very real way about very real things. I began to believe that life could be liberating for someone like me, a black Catholic man.

> I began to believe that life could be liberating for someone like me, a black Catholic man.

Every once in a while I think about how racism and discrimination have impacted society. I think about the limited number of TV shows, movies, and/or commercials that have black people in them. I think of how the few blacks who are in the media are often displayed in negative roles. Other blacks have roles that are not to be taken seriously or are stereotypical. Right around Oscar nomination time each year, my wife and I are reminded of how few, if any, Oscar nominees look like us. And if there are one or two black nominees, what type of role did they portray?

In our church we see plenty of statues, paintings, and portraits of people who do not look like they were born or ever lived in the continent of Africa. Yet we are told it doesn't matter what color Jesus was, that the whole human community is like the image of God, so color is not important. But if race is not important, why don't we see more black expressions of Jesus or Mary as statues, paintings and portraits in our churches? Why don't we have more information on black folks and black saints who definitely existed in early Christian/Catholic history?

Racism exists not only towards individuals, but also within institutions. These walls of discrimination must be removed and torn down by all in every way. I saw institutional racism evident when my son and his classmates, all graduates of a prominent and respected Catholic high school in Chicago — my alma mater, in fact — being harassed by Chicago police officers because they were "DWB" — driving while black. These young people strove for academic excellence, civic mindedness and human compassion. They were three of the top performing students of their class. None of these attributes was considered, however, as they were frisked and held up against a car that had merely missed its emissions renewal. As a result of this incident, my son decided he would not live here in Chicago. He has chosen to remain in his college state of Minnesota, where he feels safer and more accepted as a young black man.

Finally, I saw evidence of institutional racism through the experiences of my late brother-in-law, who was a brilliant businessman and had to fight racism all of his sixty years. He had terrific ideas for organic food development, but he could not generate capital to implement his ideas. No one thought his ideas would become a legitimate industry that they could entrust to a black man to develop. He fought more than ten years, sacrificing his health and all of his relationships to try to see this project through. He was told more than once that if he just had the right connections he could raise enough money to do the project justice. He had a wonderful concept.

My brother-in-law did not live to vote for the first black president of the U.S.A., but he wanted to. He did not get a chance to support his family as he wanted to. He did not live to see one of his nephews get married. And he did not get to see his son graduate from high school. It was racism that put the roadblock up and kept him from creating the life he had dreamed for himself and his family. Racism continued to raise its ugly head in every endeavor he pursued. However, he never accepted racism or discrimination as an excuse for his not being successful; but I witnessed it firsthand every step of the way.

I believe America is beginning to get itself ready to deal with racism in a steady and serious way. We are not there yet, as seen throughout the country as Obama was running for president. Some people were not willing to vote for a black man to be president just because he is black. Obama proved, however, that we are ready for the discussion.

Martin Luther King, Jr., hoped for the complete eradication of racism, but I believe my children will still be "judged by the color of their skin" and not "by the content of their character." They will also be judged by who they talk to in their lives and who will help pave their ways. I do remain hopeful and trust in the Lord for this world and this country to get it right.

LET US OPEN
THE DOORS

Olga Anglada

Olga Anglada is a member of the Social Justice Ministry at her parish, Queen of All Saints, in Chicago. Through the Archdiocese of Chicago, she participates in the Workshops on Racism and Ethnic Sensitivity, where she is a witness speaker. Olga has a strong belief in the principles of Catholic social teaching. She is a social worker, and her work is motivated by her desire to provide education regarding issues of social justice. She is married to her husband, Rafael, and they have two children, R.J. and Karina.

Every day when I get up I begin my day by praying for my family and, especially, for my two young-adult children. I am grateful that they are healthy, productive and terrific people.

Many times I have fear in my heart. There are times when I do not wish to tell my children what is in my heart. I do not want them to become worried or too concerned about life; but, as a mother, I worry. One of the reasons I worry comes from my own experience when I came to the United States as an immigrant. Other reasons are related to the cruel treatment I have witnessed toward people of color.

My first experience of blatant racism occurred when I decided to attend school and obtain my master's degree at the Jane Addams School of Social Work at the University of Illinois at Chicago. I began the application process by complying with all the requests — letters of recommendation, transcripts and submission of the application. It was a long and difficult experience, exacerbated by my short amount of time in the U.S. At each step, I began to question things that did not seem right. In my mind, I believed that I was in the land of opportunity. I recall how I looked forward to attending school.

But unfortunately, things did not go smoothly.

After the university reviewed my application package they sent me a letter stating that I needed to take an English test and provide proof that I was literate in English. I did not think much about the request. Since I came from a country where my primary language was Spanish and I was relatively new here, I agreed to their request. Shortly thereafter, I received all the information related to the test. However, when I reviewed the information I learned that I could not take the test if I could not provide my immigration green card. I did not have a green card, since I was an American citizen who had come to the U.S. from Puerto Rico. I remember having a big struggle with the university because they insisted that I could not apply for admission since I was an "undocumented alien" and had no choice but to abide by their rules. At that point I decided to meet the challenge and

I informed them of their ignorance with regard to my culture and country of origin, Puerto Rico.

fight back. It was my conviction that I had the right to pursue graduate studies just like any other American citizen. The review of my case was very long.

In a letter I wrote to the university officials, I informed them of their ignorance with regard to my culture and country of origin, Puerto Rico. At that point, I indicated that I had changed my mind and did not wish to attend their university. I felt they did not deserve to have me attend or have the power to make me prove my literacy in the English language and my American citizenship. A short time after one of my last letters to them, I received a response stating that I did not have to take the test or prove my knowledge of the English language. Finally, the university had accepted me. The sad part was that I had to go through much unnecessary misunderstanding and grief in the whole process.

Another incident in which I experienced hurt

because of a difficult situation was when my son had an automobile accident. My main concern was my son's safety as well as that of the other driver. When I arrived on the scene, I went directly to see my son and he was fine. I recall leaving my son to exchange information with a police officer and went to see the other young man to assure myself that he also was fine. I kept my distance from my son and went to a corner to wait for him. At the accident scene there was another male officer and a female officer off to the side. Unaware of who I was and that I could hear them, they spoke about my son in a disparaging manner. My son was returning from work late that evening when the driver of the other vehicle caused the accident by rear-ending my son's car. I overheard the officers speculate that the "Hispanic driver," my son, had possibly been under the influence of drugs (DUI) or had been recklessly driving his vehicle. They proceeded to search my son's car for alleged drugs. I could not believe what the officers had said or done. Though the other young man had caused the accident, the police claimed he was innocent and had committed no fault.

When I was in Puerto Rico, I did not have to think much about the subject of race because it was not an issue for me at that time. I grew up viewing my race as "white;" however, when I came to the United States other people questioned my race and they quickly pointed out that in this country I was not "white." I became Hispanic or Latina. There were other things that needed clarification. As an Hispanic, I needed to classify my Hispanic roots. I needed to find an Hispanic classification under the umbrella of Hispanic people. It seemed hard to believe: I had to become something else; others would define me. I was given a new identity. I had a new and different persona. These changes and transitions are part of what I have been through in my life in the U.S.

All my experiences with race have not been negative. Some of the situations I have been through I find humorous. There are moments that are sad and some that are amusing. After all, life is like that. For example, one day I was at work and two white people were not aware that I was in the same room and spoke about how we Hispanics were taking over their country. They said, "You see them everywhere; you will find them in many places." Suddenly they noticed that I was in the room, and not knowing how to react they asked, "Oh, you are here; do you speak Spanish?" I just smiled and answered, *"Si,"* and left.

As we know, everybody has a story. The stories may provide a way to connect with others, but the opposite is also true. We can become disconnected by our stories. When I was asked to share my story, I had to do a lot of reflection. As part of the process, it was important for me to take the risk or the challenge. As I reveal myself, it is my hope that it will give others my point of view and let them know who I am in connection to society and church.

I believe that we can discover new insights and have the opportunity to learn from one another. We can open our minds and hearts to new dimensions of understanding, love, compassion and faith. My intent is to make a connection that will embrace a new way of spiritual growth. By telling our stories, we can open ourselves to life-changing experiences that transform us and at the same time create a better place to live as people of faith. This is why I have chosen to share my experience. I do not share my story so that people will feel sorry for me, nor to create guilt. I do so because I see the importance in making connections. I believe that it is better to be inclusive as opposed to writing people off before we have gotten to know them. Let us open the doors of tolerance, understanding and acceptance so that we may all become better people.

ACKNOWLEDGMENTS

This book is presented with great gratitude to all the people who have been part of the Workshops on Racism and Ethnic Sensitivity — the creative priests of the archdiocese who developed phase one of the workshops, the dedicated people who organized the workshops, all the parishioners and pastors who participated, and the committed parishioners who became skilled at presenting the workshops. In addition to those whose stories are in this book, many others gave witness talks and vision talks during the workshops and revealed their personal stories. Thousands have participated in the workshops, including parishioners and pastors from eighty per cent of archdiocesan churches.

Thank you to Francis Cardinal George, OMI, for your continuous support of the workshops and your affirmation of this project. Special thanks to the Office for Racial Justice and Director Sister Anita Baird for encouraging the project of collecting these witness talks into a book.

Thank you to ACTA Publications for your willingness to join with us in publishing these stories. I especially appreciate the support and interest of the publisher, Greg Pierce.

Thank you to Sr. Carlene Howell, osf, of my Joliet Franciscan congregation, who proofread the book and provided many helpful suggestions!

Finally, special thanks to you whose stories are in this book: Yoli, Sue, Joanne, Gene, Georgina, Pat, Lupe, Frances, Joe, Deacon Dexter and Olga. Your stories have touched me over and over again. I know many others will respect what you said, be influenced by your words and be moved to tell their own stories.

Lois Prebil, osf

WRITE YOUR OWN STORY

BOOKS OF RELATED INTEREST

IN THEIR FOOTSTEPS
Inspirational Reflections on Black History
for Every Day of the Year
Daryl Grigsby

Shows how the broad span of black history—in Africa, in the United States, and around the world—has molded how we all see questions of race and justice today.
384-page paperback, $14.95

A RECIPE FOR HOPE
Stories of Transformation
by People Stuggling with Homelessness
Karen M. Skalitzky

Collected from among the men and women of Inspiration Corporation, an organization in Chicago dedicated to helping the homeless back to self-sufficiency.
256-page paperback, $9.95

A LIGHT WILL RISE IN DARKNESS
Growing Up Black and Catholic in New Orleans
Jo Anne Tardy

Recounts the author's experiences as a Catholic growing up in the 1940s and 1950s in New Orleans and her encounters with prejudice because of her mixed heritage.
110-page paperback, $9.95

FINDING MY WAY IN A GRACE-FILLED WORLD
William L. Droel

Describes the author's move to Chicago as a young adult who discovers the spiritual benefits of the close-knit neighborhoods and parishes of the city.
112-page paperback, $9.95

CHURCH, CHICAGO-STYLE
William L. Droel
Foreword by Sr. Patricia Crowley, OSB

A celebration of the history of active clerical leadership and lay involvement in the Catholic Church in Chicago.
126-page paperback, $12.95

THE MASS IS NEVER ENDED
Rediscovering Our Mission to Transform the World
Gregory F. Augustine Pierce

Examines the Catholic Mass through the lens of the dismissal, exploring how the liturgy aims us toward building the kingdom of God "on earth, as it is in heaven."
126-page paperback, $10.95

Available from Booksellers or at 800-397-2282
www.actapublications.com